One Year

Words and Images

David Robinson

Tempus fuit,
est, et erit.
Tempus fugit.
Damn and blast it!

Moontree Publications

2021

Copyright © David Robinson 2021

All rights reserved. This book or any portion thereof may not be reproduced or used in any manner whatsoever without the express written permission of the publisher except for the use of brief quotations in a book review or scholarly journal.

ISBN:

978-1-716-25238-9

For Deborah
(as always)

Moontree Publications
Barton on Sea
Hampshire, UK
www.moontreearts.co.uk

Contents

4	Urban Myth (Graffiti)
5	The Angel at Fiddleford Manor
6	New Year & The Poet Tree
7	Library
8	Nereids: Amphitrite
9	Fierce Love
10	The Mouse at the Rising Sun
11	Nereids: Galatea
12	Hope Alone
13	Regret
14	In the Attic no.4
15	In the Garden
16	Genesis
17	After the Storm
18	Nereids: Arethusa
19	Four Quarter Days: Ostara
20	Conversation with the Moon
22	Nereids: Dynamene
23	On Wilverley Plain
24	Forest Fairy 1
25	On Brighton Beach
26	Forest Fairy 2
27	Everyman
28	Four Quarter Days: Litha
29	A Necklace
30	Forest Fairy 3
31	In Plain Sight
32	Forest Fairy 4
33	A Moral Tale
34	Listening & Survival
35	Drought & Four Quarter Days: Mabon
36	Threads & Autumn Morning
37	Fungus Fairy
38	Mermaids
39	November
40	Winter Solstice
41	Four Quarter Days: Yule
42	Urban Myth (No.31)

plus
a bonus collection
of random
haiku

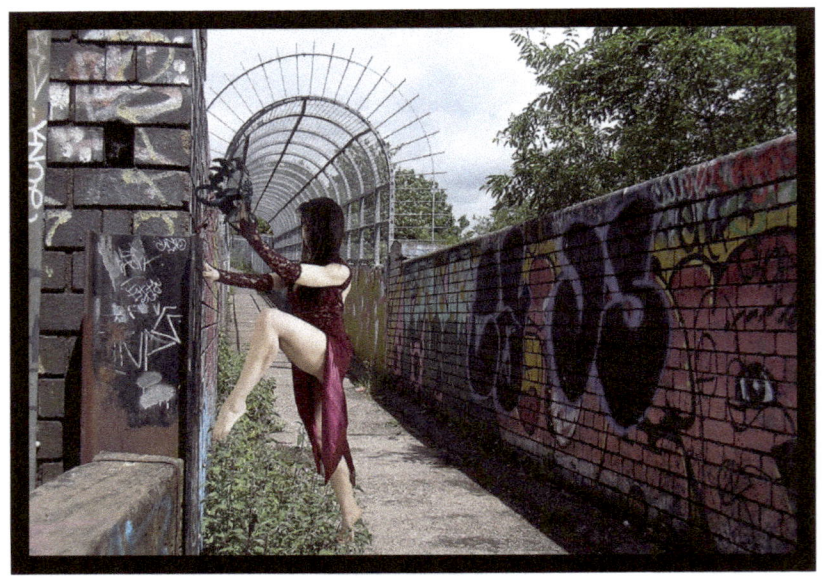

Urban Myth (Graffiti)

Six Geese
Six geese flying east
fast and low, in formation,
shouting at the sky.

      Silver Sea
     The silver sea's glare
    baffles eyes. Waves interlock
     like polished chain mail.

           Winter Dawn
         Around the curtains,
        reluctant and uncertain,
        slow winter light creeps.

The Angel at Fiddleford Manor

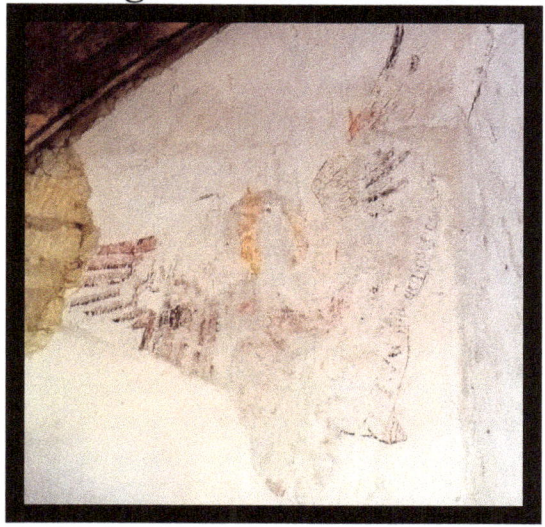

The angel watches.
The room is chill and empty.
Only now and then

strangers stand and look,
turn about, descend the stair,
leaving the silence.

After all this time
he is no longer certain
what he should announce,

or to whom. Unsure
if he had been that comet
blasting through the dark.

All those unkind years
have flaked his glory, faded
his fiery vestments,

unpicked his wide wings.
After seven centuries,
grounded and alone,

still he cannot tell
when this pale skim of plaster
might release his flight.

New Year

In January
we stand in that same doorway,
still looking both ways.

Dull eyes cannot tell
tomorrow's rash promises
from old jaded ghosts.

We stand uncertain
on this hard threshold. This door
will not reopen.

The Poet Tree

We'd like to plant a Poet Tree
in a garden, by a lake,
so we could enjoy its fruits for free.
And in its shade we'll sit and slake
our thirst with a pot of Earl Grey tea
and eat some Dorset Apple Cake.

Library

This place is full of doorways.

Silently they sit on patient shelves
in rows, just waiting for your eager choice.
And each one opens on some other world,
a world so different, or much the same,
so close at hand, but still just out of reach.

Forget your earthbound compass, fold your map,
these unknown lands are not on any chart.
Leave all your baggage on the threshold here,
step through, the weight will only hold you back.
Crossing these borders you will need
no passport, and there's nothing to declare.

And when you come back through the open door,
step back into your staid, familiar life,
what will you carry with you? What memories,
what souvenirs of terra incognita
will seed your dreams, illuminate your world?

This place is full of doorways.

Public Service Haiku #1
For the best results,
always mix your metaphors
with a wooden spoon.

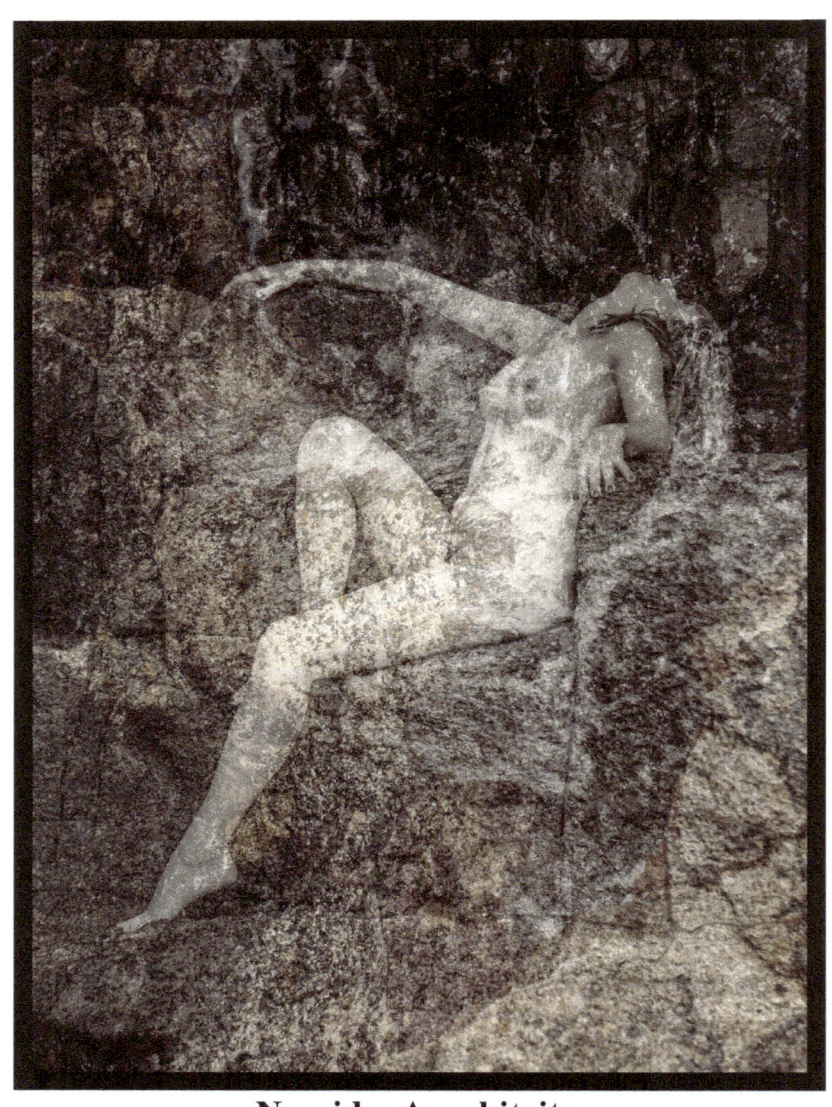

Nereids: Amphitrite

Fierce Love

We do not like to think that love is fierce.
Inside a fragile house of skin
we look for gentleness.

But love is not gentle.
It will overrun your ramparts
and leave your soul in flames.

It will lie in ambush,
take your heart hostage
and leave no ransom note.

Out of a smooth blue sky
it will cloudburst without warning
and leave you wet with tears.

Yet sometimes it will hold you,
fiercely, while you sleep, and break apart
the chains around your heart.

Public Service Haiku #2
Using similes
can be comparatively
analogical.

The Mouse at the Rising Sun

There is a mouse in New Orleans
He lives at the Rising Sun
And he's been the ruin of many a poor cat
And God, I know I'm one.

My mother was a tailor,
She sewed my new blue jeans,
But the bloody mouse just laughed at me
Down in New Orleans.

The only thing a gambler needs
Is a suitcase and a trunk.
But if you think a cat needs new blue jeans
You must be very drunk.

I've one foot on the platform,
The other foot on the train,
The mouse and his mates just point and jeer
And I just can't stand the pain.

Oh, mother, tell your kittens
Not to do what I have done,
Don't spend nine lives in sin and misery
Chasing mice at the Rising Sun.

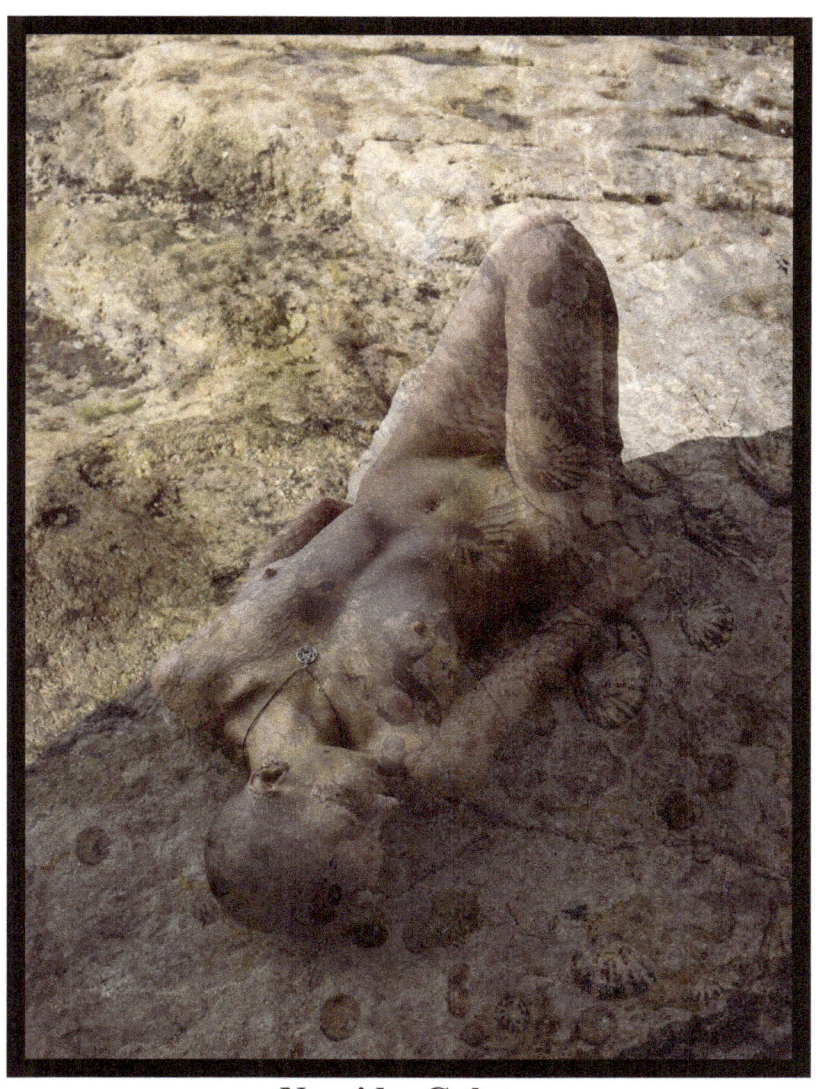

Nereids: Galatea

Hope Alone

When they made me break the seal,
how could I have known?
New-fashioned as I was, the clay
was barely dry. I could still feel
the sweaty pressure of the blacksmith's hands.

I did not choose this life.
I did not seek those tainted gifts.
I did not ask to be abandoned here.

But they could have foreseen it all.
Watching with their calculating eyes,
standing too close, their breath upon my skin.

They knew it was not me who stole the fire.

I felt them shift the blame before the act,
before the lid was levered from the jar,
before the mundane horrors multiplied.

And what did you expect?
You know the story, and the sequel:
the one about the apple and the snake.

Once your sordid pantheon of jealous gods,
conceived in your own image,
was loosed upon a naive world,
what did you think would then be shaken free?

And still you miss the point.
Within the upturned, voided jar,
wedged beneath the fractured rim,
against all expectation,

hope alone remained.

Regret

We should speak of love
but our lips have turned to rust
and our tongues to stone.
We will not bend to follow
the sinuous pull of words.

It is hard sometimes
to follow where words will go,
where they might lead us.

Down through these purblind alleys
in our shiny, splintered world
we move, distracted
by the white noise and the hum
of barren voices,

while our damaged mouths regret
all those half remembered words.

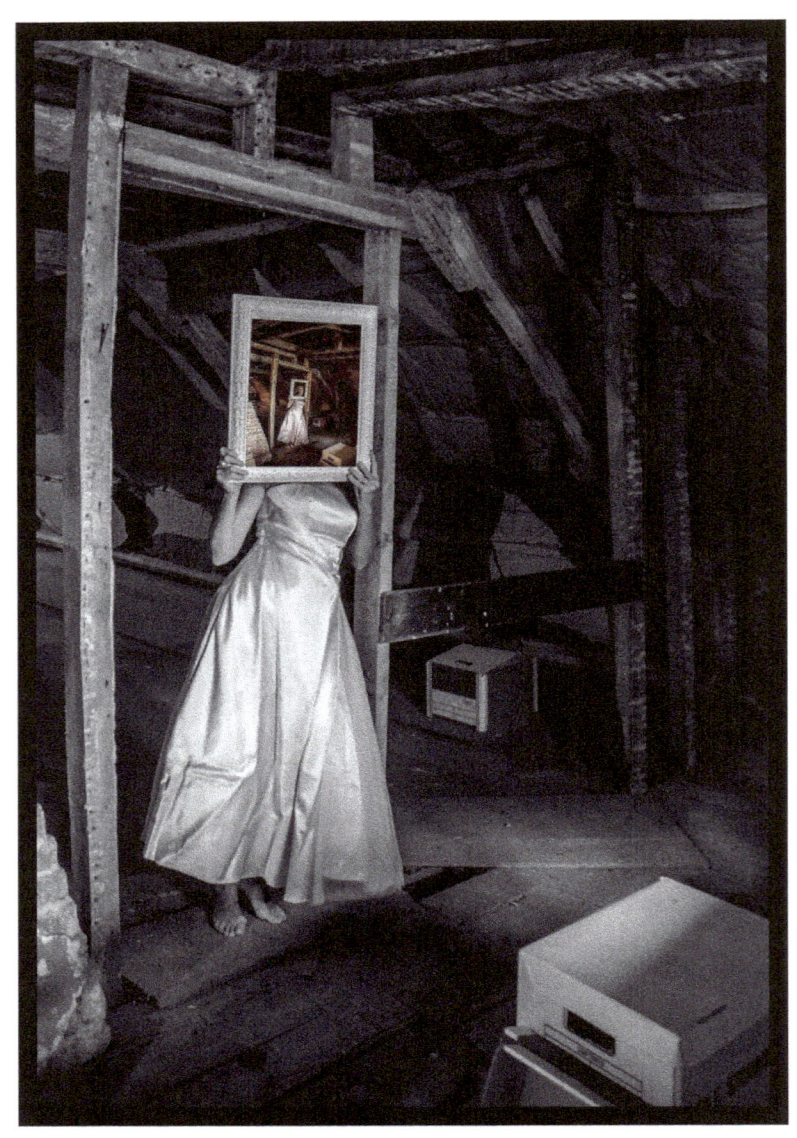

In the Attic no.4

In The Garden

No doubt you think
I should have seen it coming.

But you forget,
the world was new, the garden fruitful,
and I was artless and new-made.

They told me how
I came to be, and I believed their story,
though he would not explain,
nor let me see the scar.

And so I knew
the perfidy of serpents.
And of men.

No-one told me
there would be no way back
to innocence, or to the garden,
and no defence
against that ancient slander.

Perhaps I should have seen
the sudden hunger for a scapegoat.

Perhaps I should have known
the blame would fall on me.

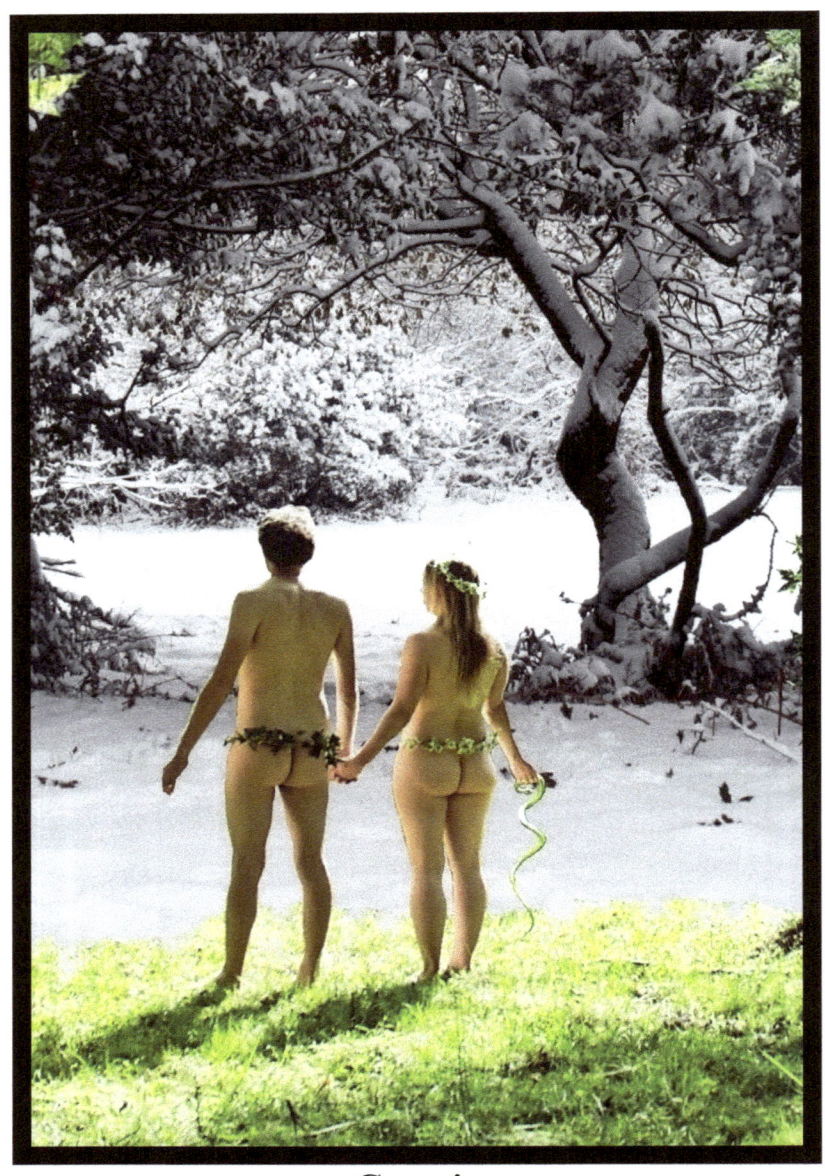

Genesis

After the Storm

Nothing will be forgotten.

The storm is over, but the sea remembers.
Beneath the hammered silver surface,
within the roaring of the undertow,
nothing is ever left to chance. The waves
swallow the seething anger of the wind,
drowning in deep green memory.

And all may be recalled again one day,
as broken jetsam washed up on the shore,
abandoned by the cold relentless tide.

Nothing will be forgotten.

The cold relentless tide abandoned
as broken jetsam washed up on the shore
may be recalled again one day.

Drowning in deep green memory,
swallowing the seething anger of the wind,
the waves are never left to chance.
Within the roaring of the undertow,
beneath the hammered silver surface,
the sea remembers, but the storm is over.

Nothing will be forgotten.

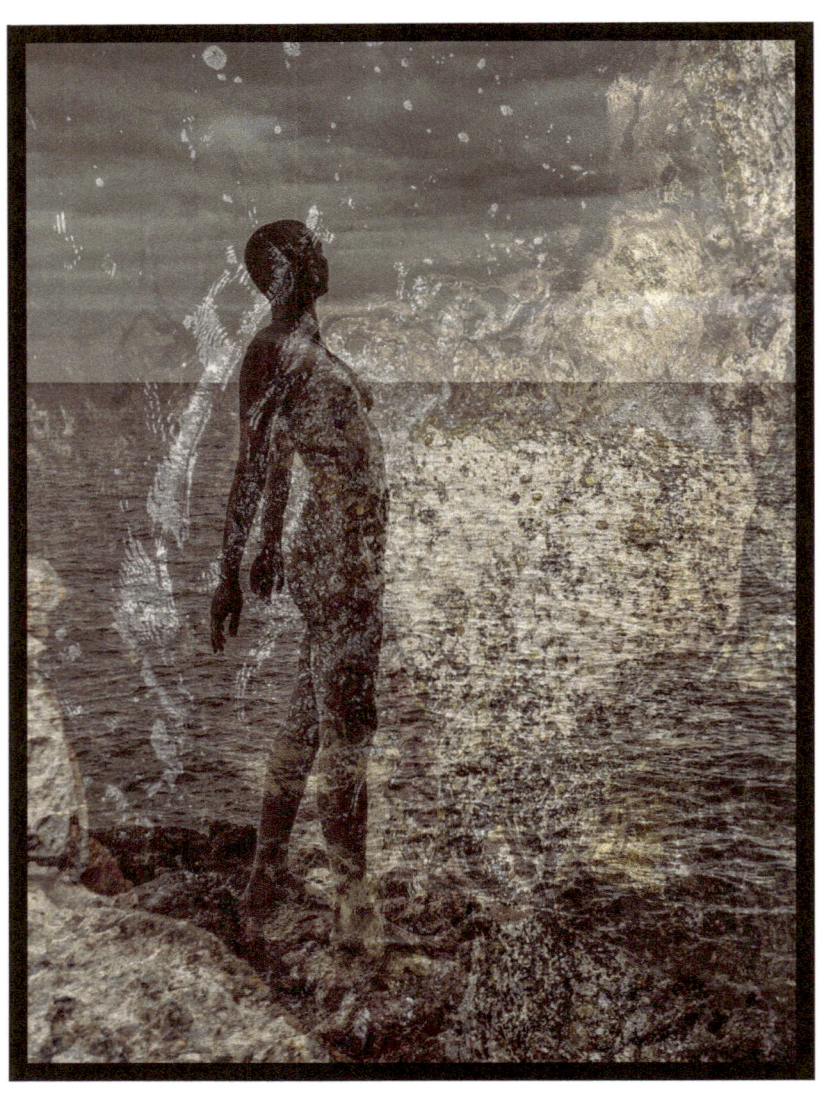

Nereids: Arethusa

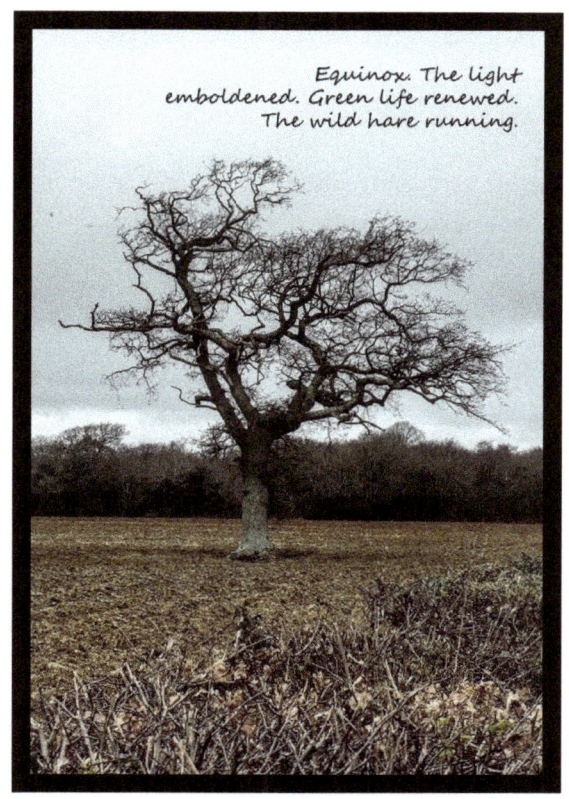

Four Quarter Days: Ostara

Public Service Haiku #3
Use a thesaurus
wisely, astutely, sagely
and judiciously.

Public Service Haiku #4
Birds of a feather
stick like shit to the wrong side
of a wet blanket.

Conversation with the Moon

Why do you walk across the night,
in this trackless dark, alone?
Listen.
You cannot anchor me here,
your feeble gravity is not enough.
Nothing will ever still me.

Why must you wear this shifting face,
with its fickle old disguise?
Listen.
Nothing will remain the same.
Change is always my constant masquerade.
No-one will ever know me.

Why do you never stay with us,
despite all our ancient prayers?
Listen.
You cannot tether me down,
your childish knots are nothing to my will.
No-one will ever hold me.

Where do you stray when not with us?
What calls to you through the cold?
Listen.
I have so many lovers
who call and yearn for me from far away.
No-one will ever keep me.

Why do you gaze down at the sea,
from your bright lonely distance?

*Listen.
I move her with my desire,
eclipsed with hopeless lust for her dark swell.
Nothing will ever ease me.*

Why do you never speak to us?
Do our old songs not reach you?
*Listen.
Listen.
I am silence. My own words
evaporate in pointless emptiness.
No-one will ever hear me.*

Public Service Haiku #5
You can never teach
an old dog in the manger
to perform new brooms.

Public Service Haiku #6
A bird in the hand
is worth two peas in a pod
and a can of worms.

Public Service Haiku #7
Don't count your chickens
before you break all the eggs
into one basket.

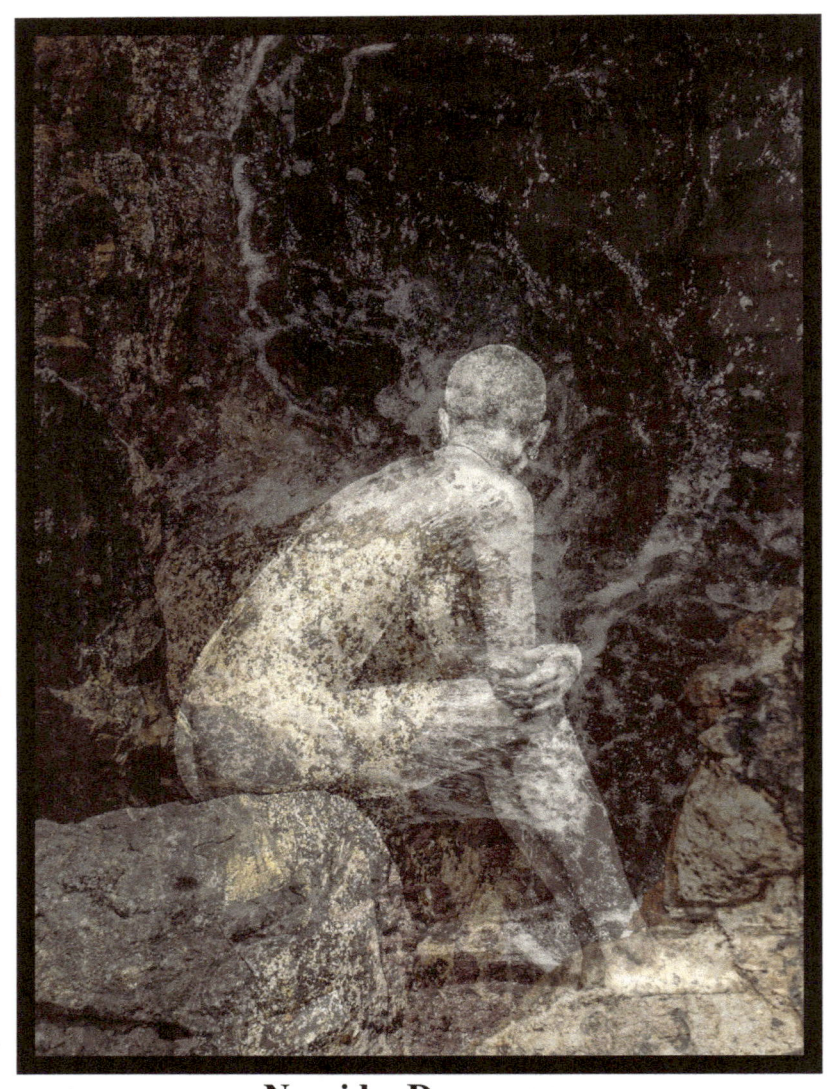

Nereids: Dynamene

On Wilverley Plain

Twilight on the plain.
A cloud of starlings flying:
a murmuration
under a three-quarter moon
spilling its pale yellow light.

Overhead, the sky
fades and then forgets itself.
In the wood, west wind
breaks surf on shingle beaches.
Bare, black branches sigh and sway.

A shadow deer stands
watching my passing, as night
trickles slowly down,
leaching colour from the land.
In the night all deer are grey.

Rooks fly home to roost.
Through the wood the path is dark,
solid dark, between
these old bones of trees, naked,
shivering in winter's fist.

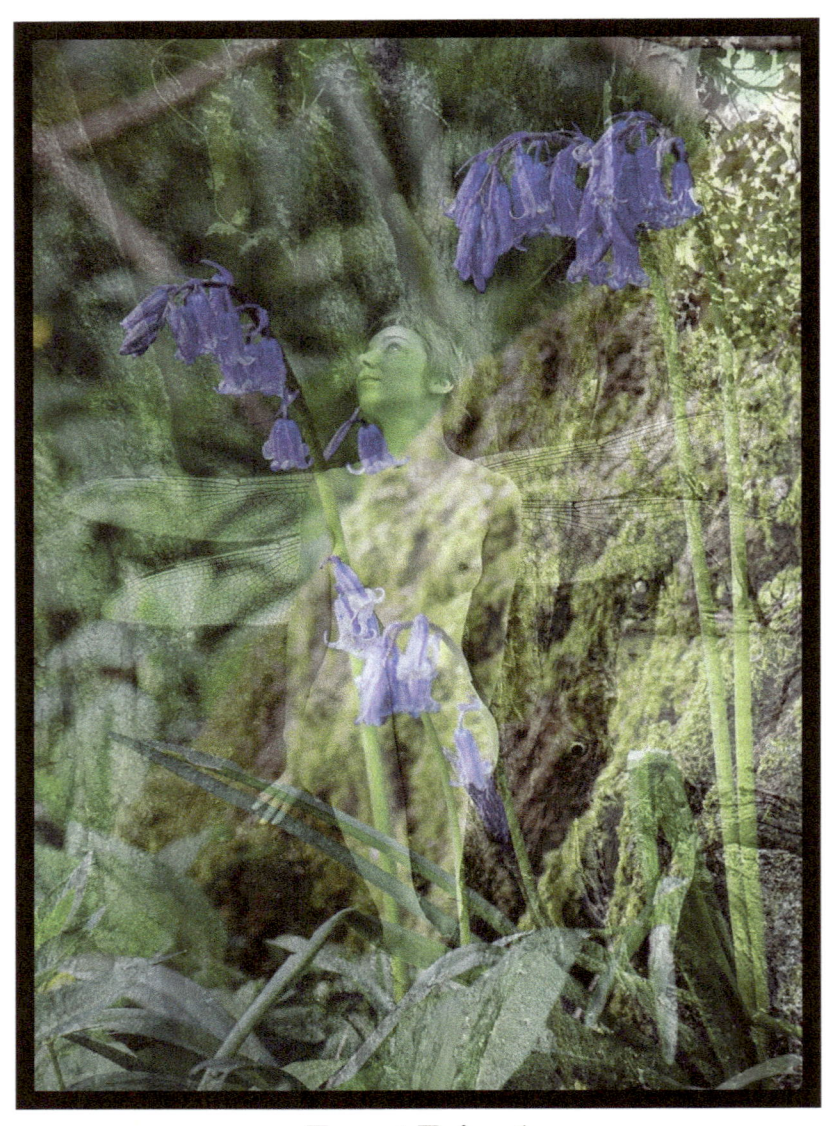

Forest Fairy 1

On Brighton Beach

I found a poem once on Brighton Beach
As I walked there all alone.
It was in an antique bottle
Half buried in the stones.

I picked it up and drew the cork
To save it from the tide.
Then I sat down to read the words,
And this it said inside:

*"I found a poem once on Brighton Beach
As I walked there all alone.
It was in an antique bottle
Half buried in the stones".*

Public Service Haiku #8
Two wrongs do not make
hay while the sun shines. Save them
for a rainy day.

Public Service Haiku #9
Your broth may be spoiled
because far too many cooks
butter no parsnips.

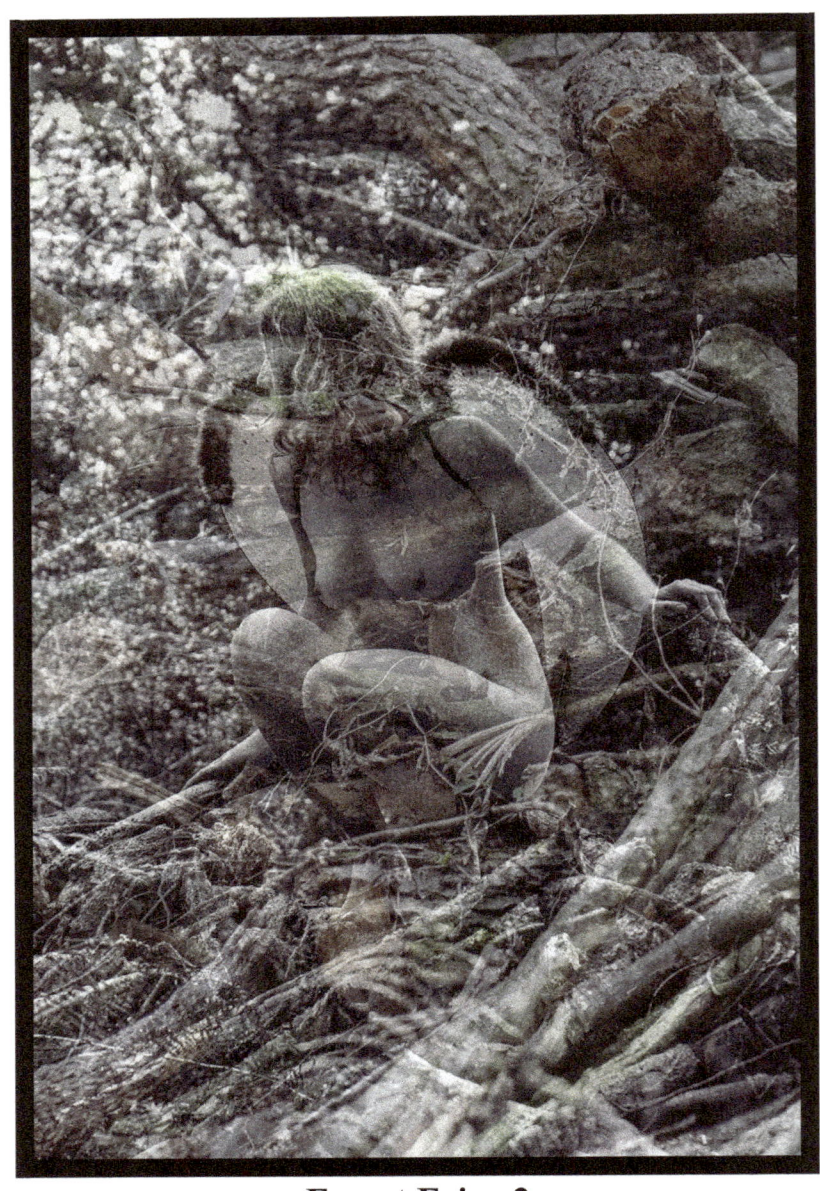

Forest Fairy 2

Everyman

In my arteries there are oceans,
in my veins, rivers.
I contain continents.

The birth of stars
is etched upon my skin.
In my eyes are galaxies.

In my loins
are all the generations that have been
and those to come.

In my bones
are all the graveyards of the earth.

And the memory of every song
from every throat
beats in my ears,
cradled on the pulse of blood.

Public Service Haiku #10
If half a sixpence
is better than no bread, that's
money for old rope.

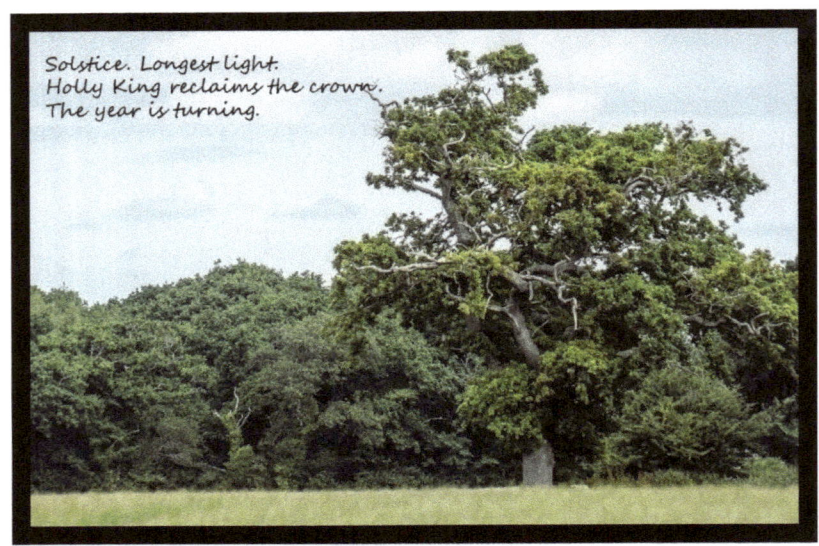

Four Quarter Days: Litha

Public Service Haiku #11
Eschew and avoid
the usage and employment
of tautology.

Public Service Haiku #12
It is said that truth
is stranger than fiction, so
let sleeping dogs lie.

A Necklace

Deep here in this close and gritty dark
the pickaxe hacks out only lead and tin.

The seam I seek is fathoms down
and deeper still. My imagined metal flows
in veins in rock, to be bled out
into perfect ingots. This silver
needs no crucible, no furnace fire,
only the baffling alchemy of love.

On my bench, the hammer and the file
shape the polished metal into charms
to hang upon a chain, every one
holding close its neighbour. Each charm becomes
a syllable that speaks its name
and knows its place in harmony.

I hang the chain about your neck.
I close the clasp, the necklace starts to sing.

Public Service Haiku #13
You can take a horse
to water, but you cannot
make a meal of it.

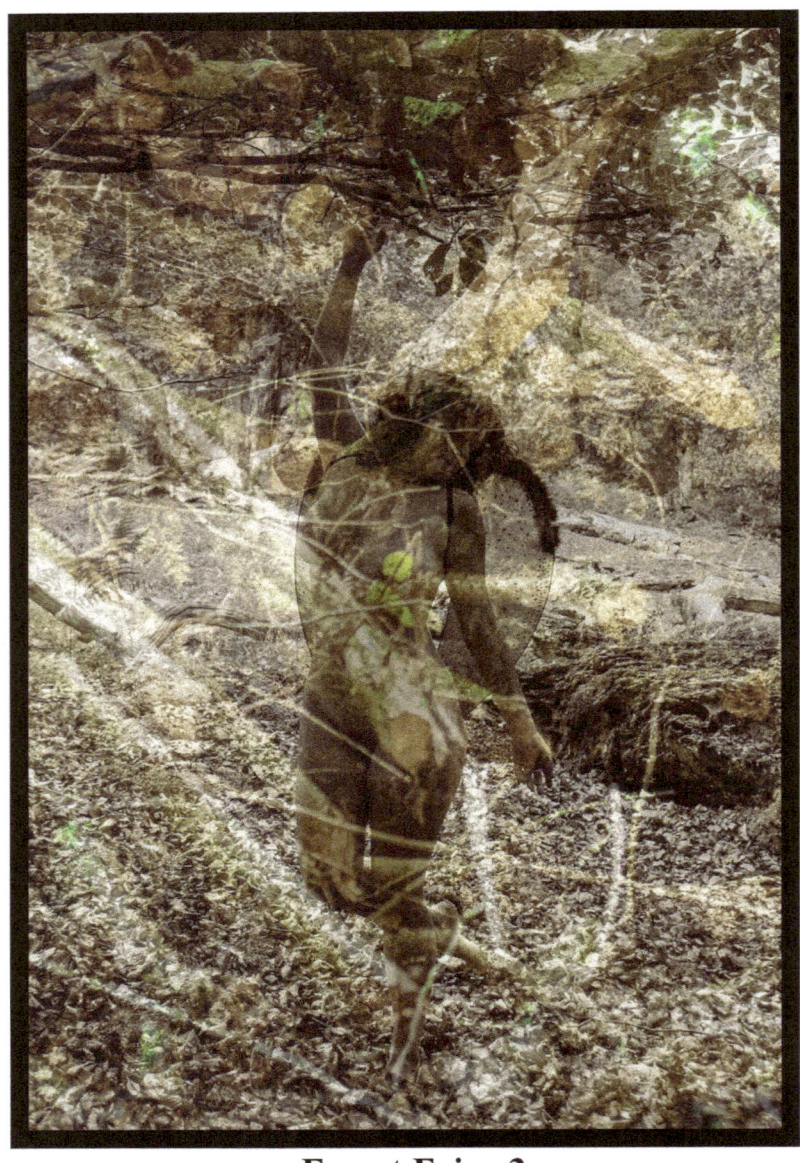

Forest Fairy 3

In Plain Sight

These crows, they do not merely fly.
Unfurling glossy wings,
they become the wind.
The liquid otter dives
and becomes the river.

Meanwhile, eyes wide, we stumble
beneath indifferent stars
that will not speak to us,
or speak in riddles only.
Although we plot their constellations
and decorate the margins of our maps,
they will not enlighten us.

When I close my eyes,
will I see everything?
The river and the wind,
the transformation of the world,
all that is hidden in plain sight.

Public Service Haiku #14
An eye for an eye
makes the whole world and his wife
look before they leap.

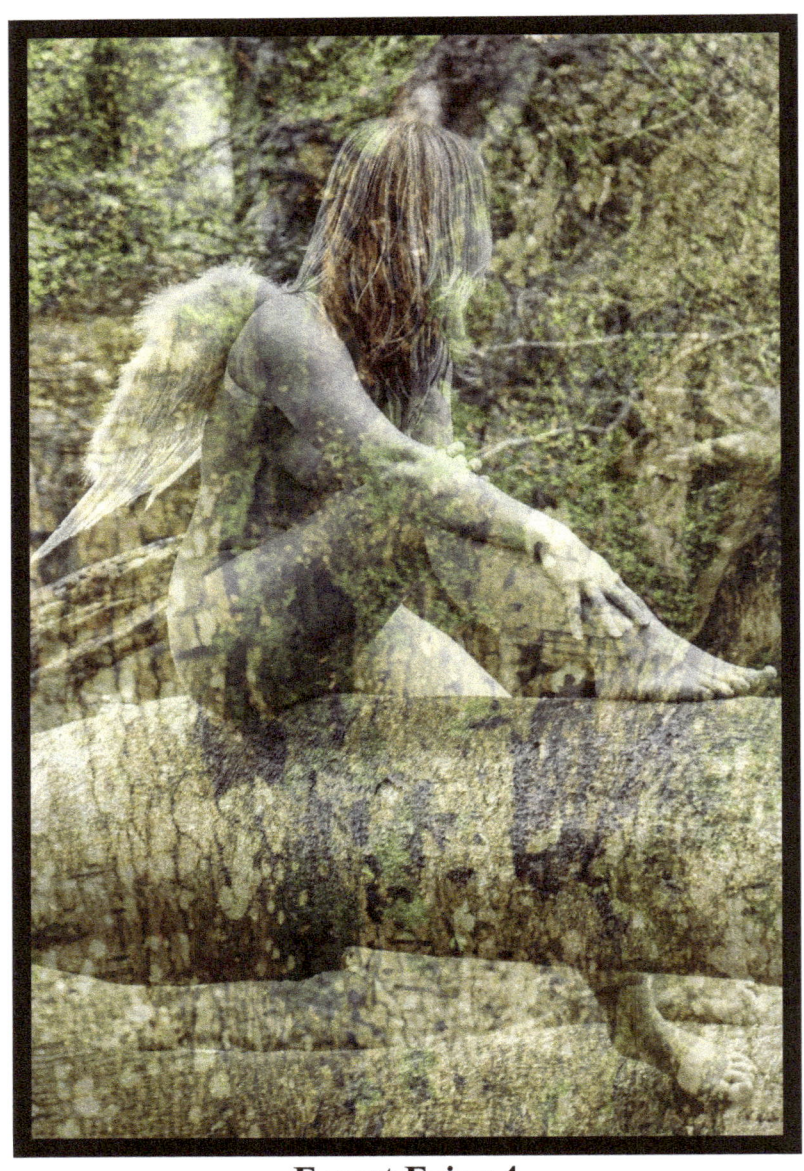

Forest Fairy 4

A Moral Tale

Batman and Robin
Had a carthorse called Dobbin
That lived in a shed near the bat-cave.
It was sort of a back-up
In case the bat-mobile packed up
And they wanted to go to a rave.

Then one day the Joker
Found a sharp stick to poke her.
Well, it ruined her day
And put her right off her hay.
It was really no joke,
It was a horrible poke.
It was frightfully cruel,
And a terrible pity
For on the way to the city
The bat-mobile ran out of fuel.

The moral of course is
One shouldn't poke horses,
And, what is far worse, I suppose,
One should never upset superheroes.

Public Service haiku #15
A watched pot never
calls the kettle of fish black.
That's a red herring.

Listening

Underneath my bed
I hear the monster breathing
like wind through treetops,

like waves on shingle.
But the wind ebbs, the tide veers
and the monster sleeps.

Sleepless, I wonder
if it ever dreams of me
lying in the dark,

listening.

Survival

We have had our cake
and eaten it too.

We have burned all our bridges
and yet we crossed them,
even as we crossed the Rubicon.

And still we paid the piper,
in his own coin,
although we always knew the devil
had all the best tunes.

Drought

There has been a drought.
In such conditions, nothing
will come of nothing.

The grasses wither,
earth cracks to dust, and paper
still rejects the pen.

Dreaming, before dawn,
words tap on dark window glass,
rain falls, and I wake.

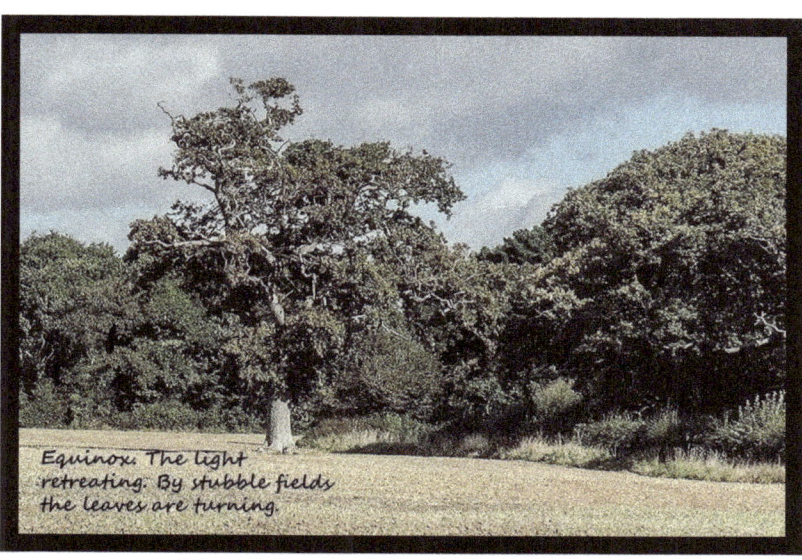

Equinox. The light retreating. By stubble fields the leaves are turning.

Four Quarter Days: Mabon

Threads

See this tapestry
whose fleeting images wind
between warp and weft.

Do not tease the threads
between your nervous fingers.
All things unravel.

Your swiftest needle
and your brightest thread will not
revive this pattern.

For once unwoven,
the loose fabric of the world
cannot be repaired.

Autumn Morning

Stiff-necked geese gather
in the mist of stubble fields
with no horizon.
Upside down in pools
the sagging sky hangs mirrored
along the salt marsh.

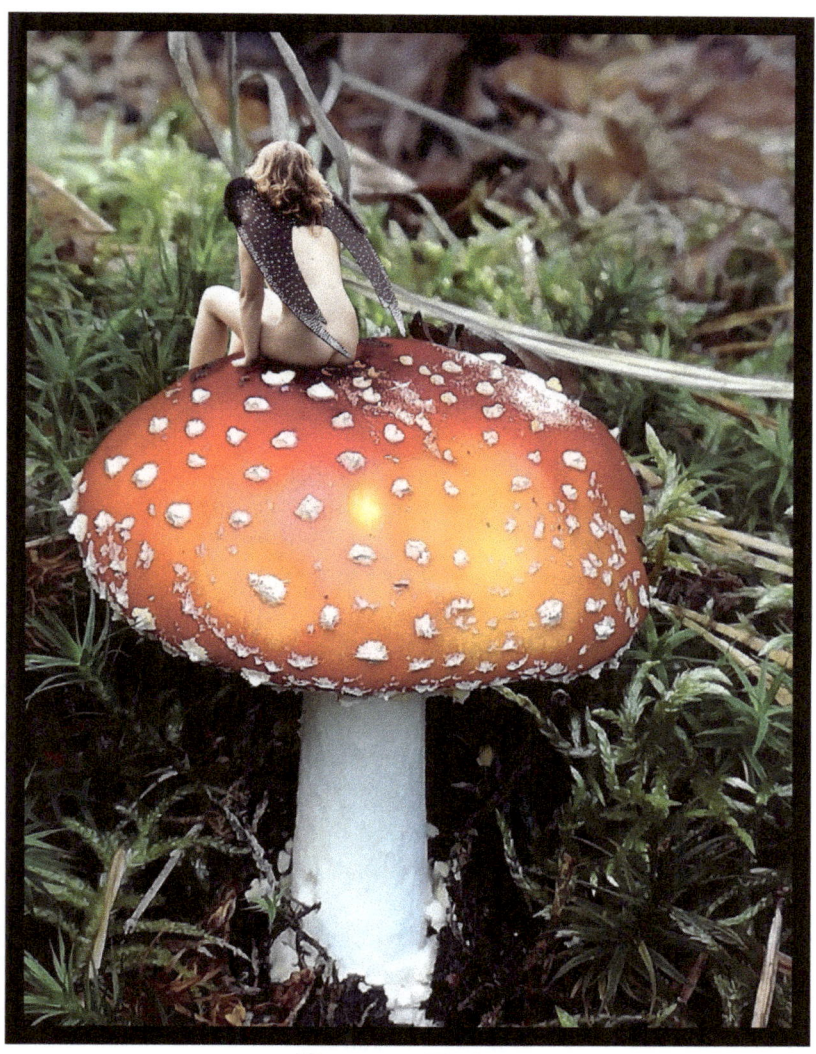

Fungus Fairy

Mermaids
(A Tragic Lesson, Caveat and Warning to Seafarers)

You landlubbers, please spare a thought
for all those jolly sailors
and captains of the whalers
by desire traduced,
by mermaids seduced,
by their siren song captured and brought
to the depths of a watery grave.

There, far below the wind and the wave,
they didn't drown, as you might have thought.
Through forests of kelp, where jellyfish play,
on tedious tides they went floating away,
not waving, not drowning,
just drifting and frowning.

As the siren's song faded
they were left bored and jaded,
for they realised too late
the sad cruelty of fate
and died of disappointment
adrift on the current.

For no friendly shipmate had warned 'em
in Falmouth or Portsmouth or Chatham
that mermaids don't have a front-bottom

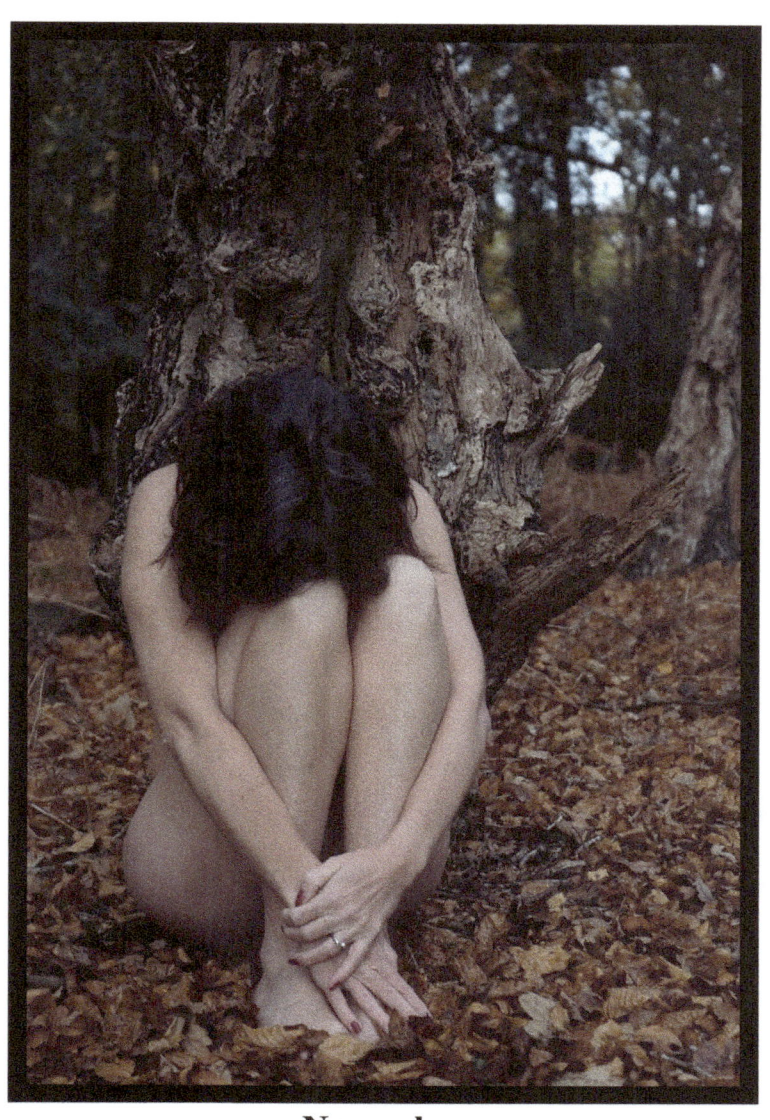

November

Winter Solstice

In this quiet wood
tread softly under winter trees.
The light is fragile and could shatter
at any moment,
between breaths, between
one thought and the next.
Yet here is the turning point,
that one brief point of balance
before, second by patient second,
the light revives.

Public Service Haiku #16
Don't flog a dead horse
of a different colour
when you're in midstream.

Public Service Haiku #17
So, if the cap fits,
I'll eat my hat. But there's a
bee in my bonnet.

Public Service haiku #18
Some clichés can be
as cool as a cucumber
or as warm as toast.

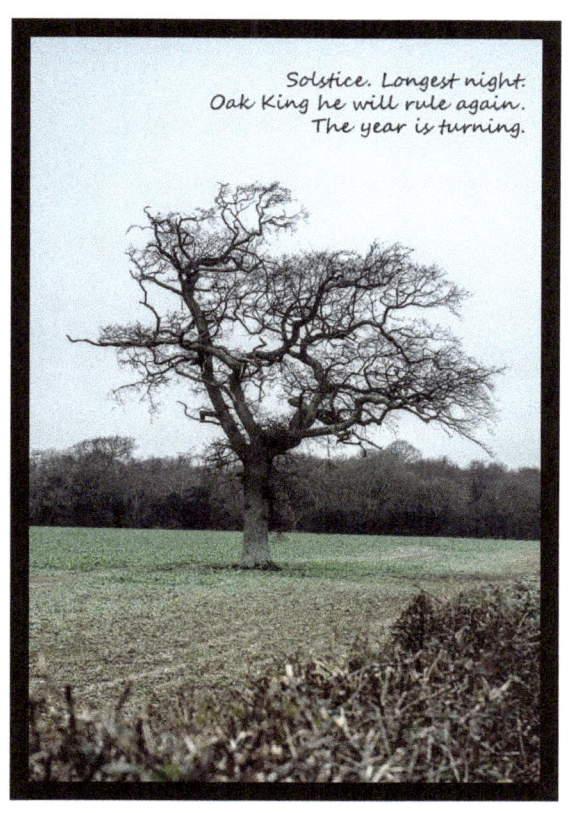

Four Quarter Days: Yule

Public Service haiku #19
You should never pull
a rabbit out of a hat
for a dog's breakfast.

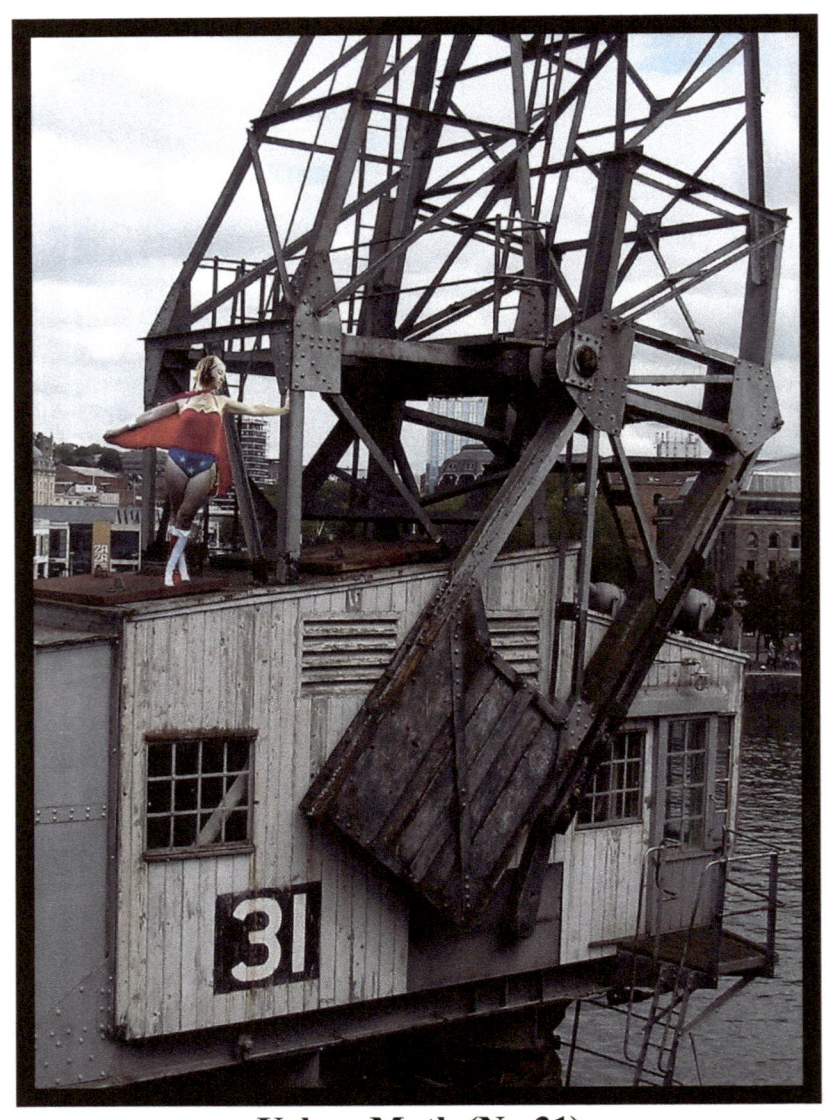

Urban Myth (No.31)

Public Service Haiku #20
You should cut your coat
to spite your face, if your nose
is to the grindstone.

Public Service Haiku #21
Please do not put off
till tomorrow what you can
ignore completely.

Public Service Haiku #22
What doesn't kill you
will probably try again.
Practice makes perfect.

Public Service Haiku #23
Bolt the stable door
once the dog in the manger
can see the rabbit.

Public Service Haiku #24
On your bucket list
should be: three buckets, a pail
and a gallipot.

Public Service Haiku #25
Every cloud has a
silver spoon in its mouth, which
leaves a nasty taste.

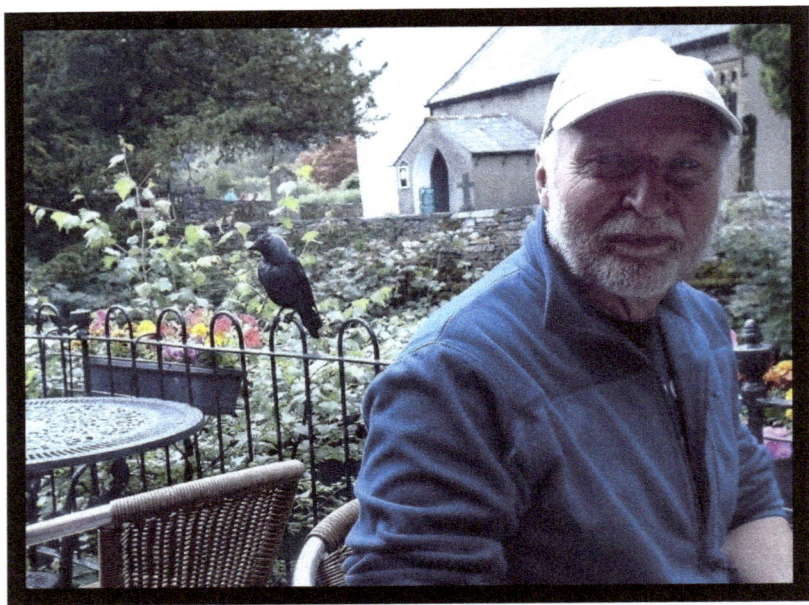

David Robinson

David is an artist/printmaker and poet and a retired teacher. He lives between the forest and the sea on the Hampshire coast, near the Dorset border.
David's visual art has been shown in galleries in Kent, Hampshire, Dorset, Wiltshire and Somerset, and in MOMA Wales.

He has produced other books of poetry and images:
"The Book of Paper Dreams" 2013
"This Deep Moment" 2015
"All That Matters" 2017
"The Adventures of Blanche" 2017
"Telling Stories" 2020

"One Year"
is a collection of poems and haiku from that interesting year, 2020.
The images are from a slightly wider timescale.

www.ingramcontent.com/pod-product-compliance
Lightning Source LLC
Chambersburg PA
CBHW040518220526
45473CB00012B/2910